VEGETABLES SCHMEGETABLES

Fun, Healthy & Kid-Friendly Foods

The Best of Dinner Table Deception

Printed in the United States of America
by G&R Publishing Co.

Distributed By:

507 Industrial Street
Waverly, IA 50677

ISBN-13: 978-1-56383-245-1
ISBN-10: 1-56383-245-3
Item #7016

TABLE OF CONTENTS

Take a Bite Out of the Healthy Eating Battle

It's a daily battle that most parents fight, getting kids to eat those good-for-you foods. Whether it's the war of the fruits or the vegetable crusade, persuading children to dump the junk and pick-up a spoonful of peas is a challenge.

The recipes in this book not only offer the healthy goodness of all food groups, but add new surprises and flavors to some of those not-so-favorite foods. In addition, enjoy some tips on table manners, recommended serving amounts, quick and healthy snacks, recipes your kids can cook themselves and information on cooking for children with special diets.

When threatening "no dessert unless you take one bite of ..." doesn't work anymore, why not try some new and inventive ways to fix healthy foods?

Tips for Picky Eaters

- Hey moms and dads, you're the role models. Set a good example by eating healthy yourself. Parents should try those new fruit and vegetable dishes along with children. Children will learn from watching good eating behavior.

- Don't expect a child to take an interest in something new the first time. Wait one week and try it again. Sometimes it takes a while for children to warm up to new foods.

- Give children a small serving of new foods. It's not as intimidating, and when finished, be delighted when they ask for more.

- Leave the junk food at the store. Offer strictly healthy foods in your home. Children will soon learn these are the only foods available to them and that's what they will eat.

Why is a Well-Balanced Diet Important?

While most parents know children need the appropriate diet to grow strong and stay healthy, there are so many other reasons it's important to maintain a well-balanced diet. According to the Center for Disease Control and Prevention (CDC), healthy diets rich in fruits and vegetables may reduce the risk of cancer and other chronic diseases. And, most are naturally low in fat and calories, as well as, filling.

Getting protein in the diet is equally as important. Younger children are at greater risk of iron deficiency due to rapid growth and increased iron requirements. To fight iron deficiency, it's important for children to eat meat, chicken, fish, whole grains, enriched bread and cereal, dark green vegetables and beans.

Just How Much is Enough?

According to the CDC, U.S. Department of Health and the U.S. Department of Agriculture (USDA) the daily amount of fruits and veggies to be consumed varies by age, sex and amount of physical activity. The following serving amounts are based on children who are moderately active, or active for 30 to 60 minutes per day.

Recommended Daily Servings of Fruits & Vegetables for Moderately Active Children

Sex	Age	Fruits	Vegetables
Girls	2-3 years	1 Cup	1 Cup
Boys	2-3 years	1 Cup	1 Cup
Girls	4-8 years	1½ Cups	1½ Cups
Boys	4-8 years	1½ Cups	1½ Cups
Girls	9-13 years	1½ Cups	2 Cups
Boys	9-13 years	1½ Cups	2½ Cups

For a more complete guide of recommended servings, the USDA's food pyramid is designed to create a personalized plan and diet. Log on to www.MyPyramid.gov for more information.

Teaching Tots Table Manners

Dinnertime can be fun and fulfilling, but also a great time for learning. Although many parents believe they have a firm grasp on their own social graces, have they even begun to think about their child's table manners? Well, it's never too early to start. Table manners can be fun, encourage self-confidence and build self-esteem. Also, good manners can be handy in more than one social situation.

Let kids know that table manners mean more than proper and polite eating, but are also about being considerate of others.

Here are some simple starters to teach children when it comes to manners.

- Eat with a fork unless the food is meant to be eaten with the fingers, like French fries or pizza. Remind children that grown-ups use utensils, only babies use their fingers.

- Those at the dinner table should wait until the host or hostess is seated and eating before taking a bite.

- Don't bite off more than you can chew. Not only does taking large bites look disgusting, but a mouth full of food could result in someone choking.

- Chew with the mouth closed and don't talk when the mouth is full. People don't want to see half-chewed food and they can't understand someone with a full mouth anyway.

- Refrain from making rude comments about the food being served. Someone worked very hard to make it and rude comments or faces might hurt their feelings. Simply say "no thank you," if it's not a desired dish.

- Don't reach across the table for a dish. Someone's eating might be interrupted, or food could be spilled. Instead, ask for the dish to be passed.

- "Please" and "thank you" can never be overused, especially when speaking to the cook. Remember to thank the person who prepared the meal for all their hard work.

- Double dipping is a definite no-no. One chip, vegetable or cracker per dip in the bowl. Double dipping is not only a yucky habit, but can spread unwanted germs.

- "Mabel, Mabel, strong and able, keep your elbows off the table." Once food is served and everyone is eating, one hand should be in the lap and the other using a utensil. It's okay to rest arms on the table between courses and once everyone is finished eating.

Tooty Fruity Recipes

CHERRYIFIC APPLES

3 apples, cored and sliced
1 C. unsweetened cherries
1 tsp. ground cinnamon

2 tsp. sugar
2 T. water

In a large microwave-safe container, place sliced apples, cherries, cinnamon, sugar and water. Mix well. Microwave on full power for 6 to 8 minutes or until apples are tender. Let stand for 5 minutes. Serve warm in individual dessert dishes.

WATERMELON PIZZA

1 (10″ thick) watermelon
  circular slice
1 C. strawberry jam
½ C. banana slices
½ C. grape halves

1 kiwi, sliced
½ C. mandarin orange sections
½ C. blueberries
½ C. pineapple chunks

Drain watermelon slice on paper towels to remove excess moisture. Spread the jam over the watermelon. Cut watermelon into triangle-shaped slices, like a pizza. Use assorted fruits as toppings or let each person create their own special piece.

GREEN APPLE SALAD

4 tart green apples, sliced
¼ C. blanched slivered almonds, toasted*

¼ C. dried cranberries
¼ C. dried chopped cherries
1 (8 oz.) container vanilla yogurt

In a medium bowl, stir together the apples, almonds, cranberries, cherries and yogurt until evenly coated.

*To toast, place slivered almonds in a single layer on a baking sheet. Bake at 350° for 10 minutes or until almonds are golden brown.

CRAZY CANTALOUPE POPS

4 C. cubed cantaloupe
¼ C. sugar
2 T. lemon juice
1 T. chopped fresh mint
   or 1 tsp. dried mint

½ tsp. grated lemon peel
12 (3 oz.) plastic cups or
   popsicle molds
12 popsicle sticks

In a blender or food processor, combine the cubed cantaloupe, sugar, lemon juice, mint and lemon peel. Cover and blend until smooth. Pour ¼ cup of the blended mixture into each cup or mold and insert popsicle sticks. Freeze until firm.

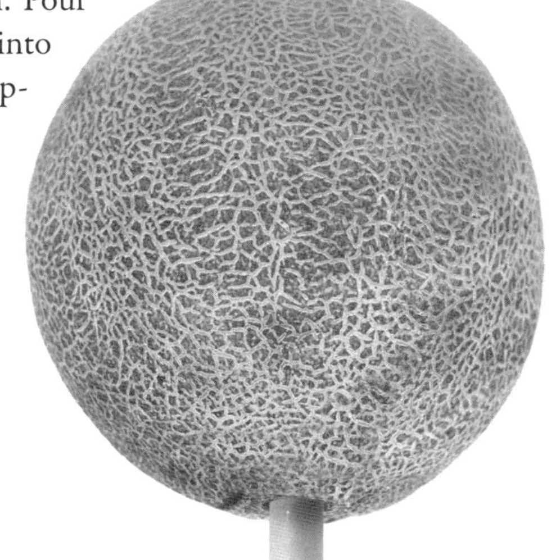

FANTASTIC PINEAPPLE FROSTY

½ C. buttermilk
¾ C. sugar
1 (20 oz.) can unsweetened
crushed pineapple

1 (8 oz.) container
whipped topping

In a bowl, combine the buttermilk, sugar and pineapple. Mix well. Fold in the whipped topping. Transfer mixture to a 9 x 13″ dish. Freeze for 4 hours or until firm. Remove from the freezer 20 minutes before serving.

BANANA MILK

1 large, ripe banana, peeled
1 C. milk
1 ½ tsp. sugar

½ tsp. vanilla
Dash ground cinnamon, optional

In a blender, process the banana, milk, sugar and vanilla until smooth. Pour into tall glasses. If desired, sprinkle lightly with cinnamon and serve.

FUN FAST FACTS
Bananas are a natural antacid, soothing heartburn or gastric distress.

TASTY TROPICAL SALAD

2 tangelos, peeled, pitted and sectioned

½ fresh pineapple, cored and cut into chunks

1 medium banana, peeled and sliced

4 T. orange-pineapple fruit juice

1 tsp. chopped fresh mint

In a bowl, mix the tangelo sections and pineapple together. Add the sliced banana to the bowl. Add fruit juice and toss gently to combine. Garnish with chopped mint and serve.

FUZZY FRUIT KABOBS

1 apple, cut into squares
1 banana, peeled and
    cut into chunks
⅓ C. red seedless grapes

⅓ C. green seedless grapes
⅔ C. pineapple chunks
1 C. plain yogurt
¼ C. shredded coconut

Slide the fruit onto skewers. On two separate plates, spread out the yogurt and coconut. Roll each fruit kabob in yogurt, then in shredded coconut until the fruit is covered. Serve immediately.

GRILLED MARSHMALLOW FRUIT KABOBS

1 ½ C. fresh or frozen
   raspberries, thawed
⅓ C. orange juice
1 T. powdered sugar
2 medium, firm bananas,
   peeled and sliced

2 C. cubed pineapple
2 large plums, cut into ¾″ pieces
24 large marshmallows
1 T. lemon juice
1 T. honey

Mash and strain the raspberries. Reserve the raspberry juice and discard the seeds. In a medium bowl, combine the orange juice, powdered sugar and raspberry juice. Preheat grill and coat grill rack with nonstick cooking spray. On 12 metal or soaked wooden skewers, alternately thread fruit pieces and marshmallows. Combine lemon juice and honey in a small bowl and brush over fruit. Grill kabobs over indirect, medium heat for 1 to 2 minutes on each side or until marshmallows are golden. Serve with raspberry sauce.

MARVELOUS MELON CONES

Seedless watermelon
Vanilla yogurt
Shredded coconut

Colored sprinkles
Ice cream cones

Using an ice cream scoop, make watermelon balls and place on a baking sheet lined with wax paper. Freeze for no more than one hour or until watermelon balls are firm. Place vanilla yogurt in a large bowl. Place shredded coconut and colored sprinkles in two separate bowls. Remove from freezer and roll watermelon balls in yogurt, then coconut and top with sprinkles. Place one watermelon ball on each ice cream cone and serve.

FUNKY FRUIT SALSA WITH CINNAMON CHIPS

2 kiwis, peeled and diced
2 apples, peeled, cored
   and diced
1 C. raspberries
1 lb. strawberries
2 T. sugar

1 T. brown sugar
3 T. fruit preserves, any flavor
10 (10″) flour tortillas
Butter-flavored cooking spray
2 C. cinnamon and
   sugar mixture

Preheat oven to 350°. In a large bowl, combine diced kiwis, apples, raspberries, strawberries, sugar, brown sugar and preserves. Mix well. Cover and chill in the refrigerator for at least 15 minutes. Coat 1 side of each flour tortilla with butter-flavored cooking spray and cut into wedges. On a large baking sheet, arrange tortillas in a single layer. Sprinkle wedges with cinnamon and sugar mixture. Spray again with cooking spray. Bake for 8 to 10 minutes. Allow chips to cool and serve with chilled fruit salsa.

PEACHY GRILLED PEACHES

4 fresh peaches
½ C. brown sugar
1 tsp. vanilla

2 T. lemon juice
½ C. fresh blueberries

Slice peaches in half and remove the pit. In a bowl, mix the brown sugar, vanilla and lemon juice. Stir in blueberries. Fill one peach half with some of the blueberry mixture and place another peach half on top. Seal the peach together and wrap with foil. Grill wrapped peaches for 10 minutes on each side. Carefully unwrap foil packets and serve warm.

FUN FAST FACTS
Peaches were once known as Persian apples.

SWEET HONEYDEW SOUP

1 honeydew melon
2 C. blueberries

6 oatmeal cookies

Cut the honeydew melon from the rind and chop the fruit into chunks. In a food processor or blender, puree honeydew chunks until smooth. Transfer to a large bowl and stir in blueberries. Chill in the refrigerator until very cold. Serve in individual bowls and crumble oatmeal cookies over each serving.

VERY STRAWBERRY SOUP

3 C. strawberries
1 C. half and half
½ C. vanilla yogurt

Sugar to taste
Dash of cinnamon

In a blender, combine strawberries, half and half, vanilla yogurt, sugar and cinnamon. Blend until smooth and chill in the refrigerator until ready to serve.

CREAMY ORANGE SALAD

1 (3 ½ oz.) pkg. instant vanilla pudding mix

1 ½ C. milk

⅓ C. frozen orange juice concentrate, thawed

¾ C. sour cream

1 (20 oz.) can pineapple tidbits, drained

1 (15 oz.) can sliced peaches, drained

1 (11 oz.) can mandarin orange segments

2 bananas, sliced

1 apple, peeled, cored and sliced

In a medium mixing bowl, combine pudding mix, milk and orange juice concentrate. With an electric mixer on medium speed, beat the orange dressing mixture for 2 minutes. Mix in sour cream. In a large salad bowl, combine pineapples, peaches, mandarin oranges, bananas and apple slices. Gently mix in orange dressing. Cover bowl and chill in the refrigerator for 2 hours before serving.

VEGGIES SCHMEGGIES

CHEESY SAUTÉED EGGPLANT

2 T. olive oil
4 C. cubed eggplant
  (1″ cubes)
Salt and pepper to taste

1 T. chopped fresh basil
1 tsp. crushed garlic
2 T. fresh grated
  Parmesan cheese

In a 10″ skillet, heat olive oil over medium heat. Add the cubed eggplant, salt, pepper and fresh chopped basil. Sauté until cubed eggplant is slightly browned and becomes tender, about 6 to 8 minutes. Add the garlic and cook for 1 additional minute. Sprinkle with fresh grated Parmesan cheese and serve.

FABULOUS VEGETABLE FRITTATA

1 ½ C. frozen hash
    browns, thawed
½ C. chopped onion
½ C. chopped red pepper
1 C. broccoli florets,
    cut into small pieces

1 T. margarine
1 ½ C. egg whites
¾ C. shredded Cheddar cheese

Preheat broiler. Wrap the handle of 10″ skillet with nonstick aluminum foil. In the skillet over medium heat, sauté hash browns, chopped onion, chopped red pepper and broccoli florets in margarine for 5 minutes. Spread hash browns and vegetables evenly in skillet. Pour egg whites over hash browns and vegetables. Cook until eggs are almost set. Top with shredded Cheddar cheese and place under broiler until cheese is melted, about 1 to 2 minutes.

CELERY STICKS AND CARROT STONES

5 celery ribs, julienned
2 large carrots, julienned
1 (8 oz.) can sliced water
   chestnuts, drained
2 T. olive or vegetable oil

2 T. cider vinegar
1 tsp. sugar
1 tsp. Dijon mustard
½ tsp. salt
¼ tsp. dillweed

In a saucepan, place julienne-cut celery and carrots and cover with water. Bring to a boil. Cook, uncovered, for 3 to 4 minutes. Drain saucepan and rinse vegetables under cold water. Transfer cooked vegetables to a large bowl and add the drained water chestnuts. In a small bowl, whisk together oil, vinegar, sugar, mustard, salt and dillweed. Pour mixture over vegetables and toss to coat.

FORGET FRIES BAKED POTATO STRIPS

3 large baking potatoes	2 T. grated Parmesan cheese
2 egg whites	1 tsp. garlic powder

Preheat oven to 375°. Cut potatoes lengthwise into thin, ¼" strips. Pat dry with paper towels. In a bowl, combine egg whites, Parmesan cheese and garlic powder. Add the potatoes and toss to coat. Place coated potatoes in a single layer in a 10 x 15" baking pan coated with nonstick cooking spray. Bake, uncovered, for 35 to 40 minutes or until potatoes are brown and tender, turning several times during baking time.

FUN FAST FACTS
Most of the nutrients in a potato reside just below the skin layer.

EDIBLE VEGGIE BOWLS

1 green, yellow or red pepper
2 celery ribs

1 carrot, peeled
3 T. salad dressing, any kind

Cut the pepper in half and hollow out one half, removing all seeds and ribs. Cut the remaining half into thin slices. Cut the celery and carrot into 4″ sticks. Place 1 tablespoon salad dressing in the bottom of the hollowed pepper bowl and place carrot, pepper and celery sticks on the top of the dressing. Serve immediately.

FUN FAST FACTS
Bell peppers are usually solid green,
but they can also be red, purple or yellow.

AWESOME AVOCADO AND FRUIT SALAD

4 kumquats
1 small head lettuce
2 grapefruits

1 avocado
½ C. vinaigrette dressing

In a small saucepan, bring 2 cups water to a boil. Add kumquats and cook for 20 seconds. Remove kumquats from water, pat dry and slice into thin pieces. Wash and gently dry lettuce. Tear lettuce into pieces. Peel grapefruits and remove by sections. Peel and pit the avocado and slice into small pieces. In a medium bowl, gently toss torn lettuce with vinaigrette. For each serving, make a bed of lettuce on a plate and arrange the fruit and avocado sections on top.

CRAFTY CARROT AND RAISIN SALAD

1 lb. carrots, peeled
  and shredded
½ C. raisins

1 (8 oz.) carton vanilla yogurt
4 to 6 iceberg lettuce leaves

In a bowl, mix together shredded carrots, raisins and yogurt. Cover with plastic wrap and chill in the refrigerator for 15 minutes. Toss before serving and spoon mixture over lettuce leaves. Serve immediately.

EASY EGGPLANT BAKE

1 eggplant, peeled and
    cut into ¼″ strips
Salt to taste

1 (26 oz.) jar spaghetti sauce
2 C. shredded mozzarella cheese
1 C. artichoke hearts, optional

Place eggplant strips on paper towels. Sprinkle salt generously over eggplant strips and let sit for 20 minutes. Rinse thoroughly to remove extra salt. In an 8″ square microwave-safe dish, spread ½ cup spaghetti sauce. Cover with a layer of eggplant strips, followed by another ½ cup of sauce, ½ cup cheese and ½ cup drained artichoke hearts. Repeat layers once more and top with remaining sauce and cheese. Place in the micro-wave and cook on full power for 15 minutes. Rotate the dish halfway through cooking time. Let cool for 5 minutes and serve.

BREADED VEGGIE STICKS

½ C. seasoned bread crumbs
2 T. grated Parmesan cheese
¼ tsp. garlic powder
3 medium zucchinis

½ C. milk or water
1 C. spaghetti sauce or
   ranch dressing

Preheat the oven to 450°. Place the bread crumbs, cheese and garlic powder in a plastic bag and shake to combine. Cut the zucchinis into sticks. In a shallow bowl, place milk or water. Dip the zucchini sticks into the liquid then into the crumbs, tossing to coat. Place coated zucchini sticks on a 10 x 15″ baking pan coated with nonstick cooking spray. Bake for 10 to 15 minutes or until brown and tender. Serve with spaghetti sauce or ranch dressing. This recipe also works with eggplant and sweet potatoes.

ORANGE INSPIRED ASPARAGUS

2 lbs. fresh asparagus	2 T. orange juice
¼ C. plain yogurt	1 tsp. grated orange peel
2 T. mayonnaise	Dash cayenne pepper

In a large skillet over medium heat, place asparagus in 1 cup of water. Bring to a boil. Cook for 6 to 8 minutes, until asparagus is tender but still crisp. In a medium bowl, combine yogurt, mayonnaise, orange juice, grated orange peel and cayenne pepper. Drain asparagus and top with orange sauce. Garnish with orange slices and additional grated orange peel if desired.

FUN FAST FACTS
The first varieties of citrus were bitter and not edible.

ORIENTAL ASPARAGUS SALAD

1 lb. asparagus,
  cut into 2″ pieces
2 T. soy sauce
1 T. vegetable oil
1 T. vinegar

1 ½ tsp. sugar
1 tsp. sesame seeds, toasted*
¼ tsp. ground ginger
¼ tsp. ground cumin

In a saucepan over medium heat, cook the asparagus in 1 cup boiling water for about 3 to 4 minutes. Drain well and place cooked asparagus in a large bowl. In a small bowl, combine soy sauce, vegetable oil, vinegar, sugar, sesame seeds, ginger and cumin. Pour the mixture over the asparagus and toss to coat. Cover and chill in refrigerator for 1 hour. Drain well before serving.

*To toast, place sesame seeds in a single layer on a baking sheet. Bake at 350° for 10 minutes or until seeds are golden brown.

FRUITY CARROT COLESLAW

4 medium carrots, shredded
1 (10 ½ oz.) pkg.
    miniature marshmallows
1 (8 oz.) can crushed pineapple,
    drained
1 C. raisins
1 C. shredded coconut

⅓ C. halved
    maraschino cherries
½ C. mayonnaise
1 T. lemon juice
1 T. orange juice
⅓ C. whipped cream

In a large bowl, combine shredded carrots, marshmallows, crushed pineapple, raisins, shredded coconut and cherries. In a small bowl, combine mayonnaise, lemon juice and orange juice. Fold in whipped cream. Pour dressing over carrot mixture and toss to coat. Serve immediately.

Crispy Cracker Salad

12 oz. saltine crackers
3 tomatoes, peeled, seeded and diced
1 onion, finely diced
1 green bell pepper, diced

1 (8 oz.) pkg. shredded sharp Cheddar cheese
¼ C. mayonnaise
Salt and pepper to taste

Into a large bowl, break saltines. Add diced tomatoes, diced onion, diced green bell pepper, shredded Cheddar cheese and mayonnaise. Add salt and pepper to taste. Mix until well combined. Chill before serving.

OLIVE YOU ROASTED BABY CARROTS

1 lb. baby carrots, scraped*　　　Salt to taste
2 tsp. olive oil

Preheat oven to 450°. On a baking sheet, spread carrots in a single layer. Using a pastry brush, spread olive oil over baby carrots and sprinkle with salt. Roast carrots on top rack of oven for 10 minutes or until tender on the outside.

*Baby carrots have very thin skins and do not need to be peeled. Merely scrape the carrots with a knife to remove skin.

FUN FAST FACTS
Carrots are good for your eyes.

BROCCOLI FOREST

¼ C. plain nonfat yogurt

¼ C. sour cream

2 tsp. honey

2 tsp. Dijon mustard

2 carrots

3 C. broccoli florets

4 cherry tomatoes

3 T. fresh chopped parsley

In a small bowl, combine yogurt, sour cream, honey and mustard. Trim off ends of carrots. Cut each carrot in half and then crosswise to make four pieces. Arrange each serving by placing 2 carrot pieces in the center of each plate, forming tree trunks. Arrange broccoli around the carrots forming the tops of the trees. Arrange the cherry tomatoes at the top of the plate as a sun. Spoon dip around the base of carrots and sprinkle with parsley to make the grass.

BREADLESS BLT SALAD

1 lb. bacon	Salt to taste
¾ C. mayonnaise	1 head romaine lettuce, rinsed, dried and shredded
¼ C. milk	2 large tomatoes, diced
1 tsp. garlic powder	2 C. seasoned croutons
⅛ tsp. pepper	

In a large, deep skillet over medium heat, cook bacon, turning frequently, until evenly browned. Drain skillet, crumble bacon and set bacon aside on paper towels. In a blender or food processor, combine mayonnaise, milk, garlic powder and pepper. Blend until smooth and season with salt. In a large salad bowl, combine lettuce, diced tomatoes, crumbled bacon and croutons. Toss with dressing and serve immediately.

PUT ANOTHER EAR ON THE BARBIE

Pinch of cayenne pepper
½ tsp. garlic powder
¼ tsp. chili powder

1 tsp. dried oregano
2 T. olive oil
4 ears corn, husked and cleaned

Preheat outdoor grill to medium heat. In a medium bowl, combine cayenne pepper, garlic powder, chili powder and oregano. Add olive oil and mix well. Brush mixture lightly over each ear of corn. Wrap each ear of corn in foil or inside clean husks and secure the ends. Grill ears over medium heat for 20 to 25 minutes or until the corn is tender.

ORANGE GLAZED PEAS

2 (10 oz.) pkgs. frozen peas	2 T. butter or margarine
½ tsp. salt	2 T. orange marmalade
⅛ tsp. pepper	

In a medium saucepan, cook peas as directed on package and drain well. Add salt, pepper, margarine and marmalade and toss lightly to coat. Return saucepan to stovetop and cook until heated throughout.

TASTY ITALIAN GREEN BEANS

¼ C. butter

¼ C. Italian dressing

1 lb. fresh green beans, rinsed and trimmed

In a large skillet over medium heat, melt butter. Stir in Italian dressing and green beans. Cover skillet and cook for 25 minutes, stirring often. Uncover skillet and continue to heat until green beans reach desired tenderness.

FUN FAST FACTS

During the festival of Setsuben in Japan, beans are scattered in dark corners and entrances of the home to drive out evil spirits.

SNAPPY SNACKS

FROSTED WATERMELON SHAPES

Seedless watermelon, cut in ¾″ slices

Vanilla yogurt
Granola

Use cookie cutters to cut shapes out of the watermelon slices. Spread vanilla yogurt over the watermelon shapes and sprinkle with granola. Serve immediately.

WATERMELON DIP STICKS

1 C. sour cream

¼ C. sugar

1 tsp. vanilla

Watermelon, cut into wedges

In a small bowl, blend together the sour cream, sugar and vanilla. Mix until well combined. Serve mixture as dip for the watermelon wedges.

BAKED POTATO CHIPS

2 large russet potatoes,
   sliced into ⅛″ thick rounds
2 T. olive oil

1 tsp. dried thyme
½ tsp. coarse salt

Preheat oven to 400°. Do not peel the potatoes. In a large bowl, combine potato rounds, olive oil and dried thyme. Toss until evenly coated. On 2 nonstick baking sheets, arrange potatoes in a single layer. Bake until potatoes begin to brown on bottom, about 15 minutes. Turn potatoes over and continue to bake until brown and crisp, about 20 minutes. Sprinkle with salt and serve.

FUN FAST FACTS
A baked potato with skin is a good
source of dietary fiber (4 grams).

DREAMY ORANGE POPS

1 (3 oz.) pkg. orange gelatin
1 C. boiling water
1 C. vanilla yogurt
½ C. milk

½ tsp. vanilla
10 (3 oz.) plastic cups
   or popsicle molds
10 popsicle sticks

In a large bowl, dissolve gelatin in boiling water. Let mixture cool to room temperature and stir in yogurt, milk and vanilla. Pour ¼ cup liquid into each mold or cup and insert sticks. Freeze until firm.

HONEY OF A YOGURT POP

2 C. reduced fat strawberry yogurt

1 (8 oz.) can unsweetened crushed pineapple

1 T. honey

2 to 3 drops red food coloring, optional

10 (3 oz.) plastic cups or popsicle molds

10 popsicle sticks

In a blender or food processor, combine yogurt, crushed pineapple, honey and food coloring. Cover and process until smooth. Pour ¼ cup of the mixture into each mold or cup and insert sticks. Freeze until firm.

Sweet and Spicy Popcorn

4 qts. air-popped popcorn
3 T. butter
¼ C. sugar

1 T. water
1 tsp. ground cinnamon
¼ tsp. salt

Preheat oven to 300°. Place the popcorn in a large roasting pan coated with nonstick cooking spray. In a medium saucepan over low heat, melt butter. Add sugar, water, cinnamon and salt. Cook and stir until sugar is dissolved. Pour mixture over popcorn and toss until evenly coated. Bake, uncovered, for 10 to 15 minutes. Serve immediately.

VERY BERRY SMOOTHIES

⅔ C. milk
¾ C. frozen unsweetened
    strawberries
⅓ C. frozen unsweetened
    raspberries

2 T. sugar
¾ C. ice cubes

In a blender or food processor, process the milk, strawberries, raspberries and sugar until blended. Add ice cubes, cover and blend until smooth. Pour smoothies into chilled glasses and serve immediately

FUN FAST FACTS

Strawberries are a great source of vitamin C, potassium and antioxidants.

AWESOME APPLE TOAST

<table>
<tr><td>1 T. butter</td><td>1 large apple, cored
and thinly sliced</td></tr>
<tr><td>4 slices white or
whole wheat bread</td><td>1 T. ground cinnamon</td></tr>
</table>

Set oven to broil. Spread butter on one side of each slice of bread. Place apple slices on buttered side of each bread slice. Sprinkle cinnamon over apples. Place bread slices on a baking sheet. Place under broiler until toasted, about 2 minutes.

CHEESE STICKS

1 (8 oz.) pkg. shredded
   Cheddar cheese
½ C. butter, softened

1 C. flour
¼ tsp. salt

Preheat oven to 450°. In a mixing bowl, combine shredded Cheddar cheese and butter. Blend in the flour and salt. Form the mixture into 6 balls. Roll the balls into slender sticks. Cut each stick into 4 pieces. Place cheese sticks on a greased baking sheet. Bake for 8 minutes or until golden brown.

Sweet Honey Snack Mix

5 C. honey graham cereal
3 C. bear-shaped
    graham cookies
2 C. crushed Ramen noodles
¾ C. sliced almonds

1 C. golden raisins
⅓ C. butter
⅓ C. honey
1 tsp. orange juice

Preheat oven to 375°. In a large bowl, mix honey graham cereal, bear-shaped graham cookies, Ramen noodles, almonds and raisins. In a small saucepan over low heat, melt butter and blend in honey and orange juice. Pour melted mixture over cereal mixture and toss to coat. Spread mixture evenly onto a large baking sheet and bake for 10 minutes.

SPICY PRETZELS

1 tsp. ground cayenne pepper
1 tsp. lemon pepper
1 ½ tsp. garlic salt
1 (1 oz.) pkg. dry ranch
  dressing mix

¾ C. vegetable oil
2 (15 oz.) pkgs. mini pretzels

In a small bowl, mix together cayenne pepper, lemon pepper, garlic salt, dressing mix and vegetable oil. Place pretzels in a large, sealable plastic bag. Pour in seasoning mixture and shake well. Allow pretzels to marinate in the mixture for 2 hours before serving. Shake occasionally to maintain coating. Place pretzels on paper towels to drain before serving.

GOOEY CARAMEL PRETZELS

2 (15 oz.) pkgs. mini pretzels
2 C. mixed nuts
1 C. butter

2 C. brown sugar
½ C. light corn syrup
Pinch of salt

Preheat oven to 250°. In a 9 x 13″ baking dish, combine the pretzels and nuts and set aside. In a large saucepan, combine butter, brown sugar, corn syrup and salt. Stir together over medium heat until brown sugar dissolves. Bring to a boil and cook until mixture is very thick and at the "firm ball" stage (260°F). Carefully pour hot mixture over pretzels and nuts and mix together. Spread mixture onto a greased baking sheet. Bake for 20 minutes, stirring after 10 minutes. Remove from oven and spread on wax paper to cool.

LIVELY LEMON WAFERS

2 (6″) pita breads	3 T. poppy seeds
2 T. lemon-flavored olive oil	3 T. kosher salt

Preheat oven to 300°. Cut each pita into 6 equal triangles. Open each triangle and cut in half along the seam to make 2 triangles. Place the triangles, split side up, on a baking sheet. Lightly brush each triangle with lemon olive oil. Sprinkle with poppy seeds and salt. Bake for 15 minutes or until golden and crisp.

FUN FAST FACTS
British sailors used to be called "limeys" because they ate citrus to prevent scurvy on long sea voyages.

TACO BITES

1 (8 oz.) pkg. cream
   cheese, softened
1 (16 oz.) container sour cream

1 (1 ¼ oz.) pkg. taco
   seasoning mix
10 (10″) flour tortillas

In a medium mixing bowl, blend together cream cheese and sour cream. Mix in taco seasoning. Spread some of the mixture over each tortilla. Stack the tortillas 5 high, with the mixture layered between them. Cover and refrigerate overnight. Cut into wedges and serve.

PINEAPPLE YOGURT CAKES

½ C. vanilla yogurt

¼ C. crushed pineapple, drained

⅛ tsp. ground cinnamon

8 mini rice cakes

In small bowl, combine vanilla yogurt, crushed pineapple and cinnamon. Mix well. Cover and store in refrigerator for up to 1 week. Spread ½ tablespoon of yogurt mixture over each mini rice cake. If desired, top with various fruits, such as strawberries, mandarin oranges, pineapple tidbits, bananas or kiwi.

STRAWBERRY BARS

1 C. flour
1 C. rolled oats
½ C. butter or
    margarine, softened

⅓ C. brown sugar
¼ tsp. baking powder
⅛ tsp. salt
¾ C. strawberry jam

Preheat oven to 350°. In a large bowl, combine flour, oats, butter, brown sugar, baking powder and salt. Press 2 cups of the mixture into the bottom of an 8″ square baking dish. Using a large spoon, spread strawberry jam evenly over oats layer. Sprinkle the remaining oat mixture over the strawberry jam. Press down lightly. Bake for 25 minutes, remove from oven and allow to cool for at least 15 minutes before cutting into squares.

COOL AS A CUCUMBER DIP

1 C. sour cream
1 C. mayonnaise
1 T. dried minced onion
2 T. dried parsley
2 tsp. dried dillweed

2 tsp. Beau Monde seasoning
¼ tsp. seasoning salt
⅛ tsp. pepper
1 cucumber, sliced

In a medium bowl, mix sour cream, mayonnaise, dried onion, dried parsley, dillweed, Beau Monde seasoning, seasoning salt and pepper. Mix well, cover and chill in refrigerator for up to 8 hours before serving with sliced cucumber.

BRAINY BREAKFAST

FRENCH TOAST BAKE

1 (1 lb.) loaf French bread,
   cut diagonally into 1″ slices
8 eggs
2 C. milk
1 ½ C. half and half

2 tsp. vanilla
¼ tsp. ground cinnamon
¾ C. butter
1 ⅓ C. brown sugar
3 T. light corn syrup

Grease a 9 x 13″ baking dish and arrange bread slices evenly across bottom. In a large bowl, beat together eggs, milk, half and half, vanilla and cinnamon. Pour mixture over bread slices, cover and refrigerate overnight. The next morning, preheat oven to 350°. In a small saucepan over medium heat, combine butter, brown sugar and corn syrup. Heat, stirring often, until bubbling. Pour over bread and egg mixture. Bake, uncovered, for 40 minutes.

BREAKFAST PIE

¾ lb. breakfast sausage
2 T. minced onion
2 T. minced green bell pepper
1 (12 oz.) can refrigerated
  biscuit dough

3 eggs, beaten
3 T. milk
½ C. shredded Colby-Monterey
  Jack cheese

Preheat oven to 400°. In a large skillet over medium heat, combine sausage, onion and green pepper. Cook until sausage is evenly browned. Drain, crumble and set aside. Separate the dough into 10 individual biscuits. Flatten each biscuit out and press 1 biscuit into bottom and up the sides of each of 10 muffin cups. Distribute the sausage mixture between the cups. In a small bowl, whisk together the eggs and milk. Divide mixture evenly between the cups. Sprinkle tops with shredded cheese. Bake for 18 to 20 minutes or until filling is set.

FUN FAST FACTS
Eat onions to fight insomnia.
Onions contain a mild
natural sedative called quercetin.

BANG-UP BREAKFAST TORTILLA

2 T. refried beans
2 T. salsa
3 eggs, beaten

1 T. mayonnaise
4 (6″) flour tortillas
1 ½ C. shredded lettuce

In a small bowl, mix together refried beans and salsa. Place a medium, nonstick skillet over medium heat. Pour beaten eggs into pan and allow bottom to set for 1 minute. Spread bean mixture over half of the eggs and flip other half over to make a half-circle. Continue to cook until eggs are set. Spread an equal amount of mayonnaise onto each tortilla. Cut the eggs into 4 equal pieces and place 1 piece on each tortilla. Cover each with shredded lettuce, roll up and serve.

WONDERFUL APPLE PIE WAFFLE

1 ¾ C. whole wheat flour	2 tsp. active dry yeast
½ C. wheat bran	2 medium apples, grated
½ tsp. salt	3 T. applesauce
1 tsp. apple pie spice	1 C. milk
¾ C. water	2 egg whites
1 tsp. honey	

In a medium bowl, stir together whole wheat flour, wheat bran, salt and apple pie spice. Mix well and set aside. In a separate bowl, stir together water and honey. Sprinkle yeast over the surface of the water mixture and let stand for 5 minutes to dissolve. When the yeast has dissolved, stir in the grated apples, applesauce, milk and egg whites, stirring until well blended. Stir apple mixture into dry ingredients. Cover and let set for 15 minutes. Heat the waffle iron and coat with nonstick cooking spray. Spoon the waffle batter onto the iron. Close the iron and cook for 7 minutes or until the steam stops coming out and the waffle can be easily removed.

MUNCH'EM MILLET MUFFINS

2 ¼ C. whole wheat flour
⅓ C. millet flour*
1 tsp. baking powder
1 tsp. baking soda
1 tsp. salt

1 C. buttermilk
1 egg, lightly beaten
½ C. vegetable oil
½ C. honey

Preheat oven to 400°. Grease 16 muffin cups. In a large bowl, mix the whole wheat flour, millet flour, baking powder, baking soda and salt. In a separate bowl, combine buttermilk, egg, vegetable oil and honey. Stir buttermilk mixture into flour, mixing until evenly moistened. Transfer batter to prepared muffin cups. Bake for 15 minutes or until a toothpick inserted in the center of muffins comes out clean.

*Millet flour is sweet and slightly gritty. It is used to give breads and muffins a crumbly texture.

APPLE OATMEAL

1 C. water	⅔ C. rolled oats
¼ C. apple juice	1 tsp. ground cinnamon
1 apple, cored and chopped	1 C. milk

In a saucepan over medium high heat, combine water, apple juice and chopped apples. Bring to a boil stirring occasionally. Stir in the rolled oats and cinnamon. Return to a boil then reduce heat to low and simmer until mixture has thickened, about 3 minutes. Spoon into serving bowls and pour desired amount of milk over each.

WHOLE WHEAT BANANA BERRY MUFFINS

2 eggs
½ C. unsweetened applesauce
¼ C. vegetable oil
¾ C. brown sugar
1 tsp. vanilla

3 bananas, peeled and mashed
2 C. whole wheat flour
1 tsp. baking soda
1 tsp. ground cinnamon
1 C. frozen sliced strawberries

Preheat oven to 375°. Grease 12 large muffin cups or use paper liners. In a large bowl, whisk together the eggs, applesauce, vegetable oil, brown sugar, vanilla and mashed bananas. In a separate bowl, combine whole wheat flour, baking soda and cinnamon. Stir flour mixture into the banana mixture until moistened. Fold in the strawberries until evenly distributed. Spoon batter into muffin cups until ⅔ filled. Bake for 20 minutes or until the tops of the muffins spring back when pressed lightly.

PURPLE MONSTER SMOOTHIE

2 frozen bananas, peeled and cut in chunks
½ C. frozen blueberries

1 C. orange juice
1 T. honey, optional
1 tsp. vanilla, optional

In a blender, puree bananas, blueberries and orange juice. If desired, add honey or vanilla to taste. Blend for 15 seconds and pour into a tall glass to serve.

FUN FAST FACTS

Blueberries are part of the same family as azaleas, camellias, heathers and rhododendrons.

EGGS IN A MUG

2 eggs
1 T. milk

1 to 2 T. salsa
1 T. shredded cheese, optional

Coat the inside of a microwave-safe coffee mug with nonstick cooking spray. Add eggs and milk to mug and beat well with a fork. Cover mug with wax paper and microwave on high for 45 seconds. Stir and cook an additional 30 seconds. Remove from microwave and stir in salsa and shredded cheese.

SUPER SIMPLE BREAKFAST PIZZA

1 (8 oz.) tube crescent rolls
1 lb. ground sausage,
   browned and drained well
2 C. shredded mozzarella cheese

4 eggs
½ C. milk
1 tsp. salt
Pepper to taste

Preheat oven to 425°. Press crescent rolls into the bottom of a greased 9 x 13″ pan, pinching seams together to form an even layer. Sprinkle with cooked sausage and mozzarella cheese. In a medium bowl, whisk together eggs, milk, salt and pepper. Pour egg mixture over sausage and cheese in pan. Bake for 15 minutes or until set. Let stand for 5 minutes before serving.

ORANGE PEANUT BUTTER BREAKFAST BARS

½ C. butter

32 large or 3 C. miniature marshmallows

½ C. peanut butter

½ C. powdered milk

¼ C. instant orange flavored breakfast mix

1 C. raisins, optional

4 C. toasted oat cereal

Grease a 9″ square pan. In large saucepan over low heat, melt butter and marshmallows, stirring constantly. Stir in peanut butter until melted. Add powdered milk and instant drink mix. Fold in raisins and cereal, stirring until evenly coated. With buttered hands, carefully press mixture evenly into prepared pan. Let cool before cutting bars.

EASY CHEESY FRITTATA

2 eggs
¼ C. shredded Cheddar cheese
¼ C. jalapeño Jack cheese

¼ C. shredded mozzarella cheese
1 T. diced red pepper

In a small bowl, beat the eggs. Pour egg mixture into a heated medium saucepan over medium heat. Sprinkle with shredded cheeses, cover and let cook until eggs are firm and cheese is melted. Carefully slide frittata onto a plate and top with diced red pepper.

FRUIT SOUP

3 C. hot water	¼ C. dried mixed fruit
½ C. raisins	¼ C. dried apricots
½ C. golden raisins	¼ C. uncooked minute-tapioca
¼ C. small pitted prunes	1 cinnamon stick
¼ C. dried cherries	2 C. apple juice

In large saucepan over medium heat, combine hot water, raisins, golden raisins, small pitted prunes, dried cherries, dried mixed fruit, dried apricots, tapioca and cinnamon stick. Heat mixture, stirring until smooth. Reduce to low heat and simmer until the tapioca is transparent, about 30 to 35 minutes. The soup should be thick and clear. Stir in apple juice and increase to medium heat. Remove cinnamon stick and pour into bowls. If desired, serve with a dollop of cream or yogurt.

GRAPEFRUIT CRUNCH

1 red grapefruit
2 T. vanilla yogurt

2 T. granola

Peel and cut grapefruit into sections. In a shallow bowl, arrange grapefruit sections and top with vanilla yogurt. Sprinkle with granola and serve.

FUN FAST FACTS

Brazil produces the largest amount of oranges and grapefruits in the world.

CRUNCHY MORNING SALAD

½ C. sliced apples
½ C. chopped peaches
½ C. halved strawberries
½ C. chopped bananas

1 T. lemon juice
2 C. instant oats
3 T. orange juice
1 C. plain yogurt

In a medium bowl, mix apples, peaches, strawberries and bananas. Drizzle with lemon juice. Stir in oats. In a separate bowl, combine orange juice and yogurt. Add the yogurt mixture to the fruit salad and toss to coat.

GINGER HONEY MELON

¼ C. honey
2 tsp. minced gingerroot
1 tsp. grated lime peel

1 tsp. grated orange peel
6 C. honeydew or cantaloupe,
cut into 1″ cubes

In a microwave-safe bowl, mix together honey, gingerroot, grated lime peel and grated orange peel. Heat in the microwave on high for 20 seconds. Mix well and set aside to cool to room temperature. Place cubed melon in a large bowl and pour honey mixture over top. Toss to coat.

SAUSAGE AND APPLE WAGON WHEEL

½ C. vegetable oil	½ tsp. salt
1 egg, beaten	½ tsp. baking soda
½ C. brown sugar	2 apples, peeled, cored and sliced
1 C. quick cooking oats	½ lb. smoked turkey sausage links, chopped
1 C. whole wheat flour	
1 C. buttermilk	
1 tsp. baking powder	

Preheat oven to 400°. In a medium bowl, mix vegetable oil, egg, brown sugar, quick cooking oats, whole wheat flour, buttermilk, baking powder, salt and baking soda. In a 9″ square baking dish, place the apples and sausage. Pour the batter mixture over the sliced apples and chopped turkey sausage. Bake for 20 to 25 minutes, until crisp and golden brown.

SANDWICH STANDOUTS AND MARVELOUS MAIN DISHES

BAKED BROCCOLI AND CHEESE

1 (10 ¾ oz.) can cream
  of mushroom soup
1 C. mayonnaise
1 egg, beaten
¼ C. chopped onions
3 (10 oz.) pkgs. frozen
  chopped broccoli

1 (8 oz.) pkg. shredded sharp
  Cheddar cheese
Salt and pepper to taste
Dash of paprika

Preheat oven to 350°. In a medium mixing bowl, whisk together cream of mushroom soup, mayonnaise, beaten egg and chopped onions. In a large mixing bowl, break up the frozen broccoli. Using a rubber spatula, scrape soup and mayonnaise mixture on top of broccoli and mix well. Sprinkle with sharp Cheddar cheese and stir. In a greased 9 x 13″ baking dish, spread the mixture and smooth top of casserole. Season with salt, pepper and paprika and bake for 45 minutes to 1 hour.

PAINLESS VEGGIE PIZZA

¾ C. pizza sauce
1 large Italian pizza shell
1 C. chopped broccoli
1 C. shredded carrots

½ C. sliced red bell pepper
½ to ¾ C. shredded mozzarella
  or Cheddar cheese

Preheat oven to 450°. Spoon pizza sauce over Italian pizza shell and place on a baking pan. Arrange chopped broccoli, shredded carrots and red pepper over sauce and sprinkle with mozzarella or Cheddar cheese. Bake for 10 minutes. Let cool before cutting into wedges.

FUN FAST FACTS
One carrot a day can help prevent macular degeneration, a disease that eventually leads to blindness.

ITALIAN VEGGIE PASTA

½ lb. ground turkey
1 red bell pepper, thinly sliced
1 T. paprika
1 (14½ oz.) can
   crushed tomatoes
1 (14½ oz.) can chicken broth

2 C. uncooked bowtie pasta
2 C. broccoli florets
1 C. cauliflower florets
½ bunch parsley
¼ C. seasoned dry bread crumbs
¼ C. grated Parmesan cheese

In a skillet over medium high heat, crumble ground turkey. Brown turkey for 2 minutes, stirring occasionally. Add red bell pepper slices and paprika and cook for 2 more minutes. Add crushed tomatoes, chicken broth and pasta. Bring mixture to a boil. Reduce to low heat, cover and simmer for 15 minutes. Remove the lid and arrange broccoli and cauliflower over the pasta. Replace lid and continue cooking for 10 minutes. Pull leaves from parsley stems. In a small bowl, combine parsley leaves, bread crumbs and grated Parmesan cheese and toss. Sprinkle mixture over vegetables in skillet. Let sit for 3 minutes before serving.

ALOHA SANDWICHES

1 (8 oz.) can pineapple slices	8 slices bread
¼ C. mayonnaise	4 slices cooked ham
1 T. mustard	4 slices Swiss cheese
1 green onion, thinly sliced	4 lettuce leaves
⅛ tsp. cayenne pepper	

In a medium bowl, place a strainer. Pour pineapple slices through strainer, reserving the juice. In another medium bowl, combine 1 tablespoon reserved pineapple juice, mayonnaise, mustard, green onion and cayenne pepper. Spread mustard mixture over each slice of bread. Alternately layer 1 slice ham, 1 slice cheese, 1 or 2 pineapple slices and 1 lettuce leaf between 2 bread slices. Repeat to make other sandwiches. Cut sandwiches in half and serve.

TOTALLY TUNA & APPLE SANDWICH

1 (6 ½ oz.) can tuna, drained
1 C. chopped apple
¼ C. vanilla yogurt
1 tsp. mustard

1 tsp. honey
6 slices bread
3 lettuce leaves

In a medium bowl, combine drained tuna, chopped apple, vanilla yogurt, mustard and honey. Spread ½ cup of the mixture over each of three bread slices. Top each with a lettuce leaf and one of the remaining bread slices. Cut sandwiches in half and serve.

FUN FAST FACTS

Fish is good for your brain. Zinc is a mineral found in fish and shellfish. Studies show that even a minimal deficiency of zinc impairs thinking and memory.

Chinese Vegetable Stir-Fry

¾ C. pineapple juice
1 T. sugar
1 T. lemon juice
1 ½ tsp. cornstarch
1 tsp. soy sauce
4 tsp. vegetable oil

1 C. broccoli florets
1 C. sliced carrot
1 C. cauliflower florets
1 C. sliced celery
1 C. chopped red bell pepper
1 C. peas

In a medium bowl, combine pineapple juice, sugar, lemon juice, cornstarch and soy sauce. Set the sweet and sour mixture aside. In a skillet over medium high heat, warm vegetable oil. Add broccoli, carrots, cauliflower and celery to the skillet and cook for 2 minutes. Add red bell pepper and peas and cook for 2 more minutes. Add sweet and sour mixture to the vegetables. Bring to a boil and cook, covered, for 1 minute. Serve hot.

AMAZING MINUTE MARINATED CHICKEN

¼ C. Dijon mustard
2 T. lemon juice
1 ½ T. Worcestershire sauce
½ tsp. dried tarragon

¼ tsp. pepper
4 boneless, skinless chicken
  breast halves

In a medium bowl, combine Dijon mustard, lemon juice, Worcestershire sauce, dried tarragon and pepper. Spread the mixture over both sides of the chicken. Place chicken on a plate and marinate at room temperature for 10 to 15 minutes. Cook on the grill over medium heat for 10 to 15 minutes, turning once.

BEST EVER BEEF APPLE POT ROAST

1 (3 ½ to 4 lb.) beef roast
1 C. water
1 tsp. seasoning salt
½ tsp. soy sauce
½ tsp. Worcestershire sauce
¼ tsp. garlic powder

1 large tart apple, quartered
1 large onion, sliced
2 T. cornstarch
2 T. cold water
⅛ tsp. browning sauce

In a large skillet coated with nonstick cooking spray, brown beef roast on all sides. Transfer the beef roast to a 5-quart slow cooker. Add water to the skillet, stirring to loosen any browned bits and pour over roast. Sprinkle the roast with seasoning salt, soy sauce, Worcestershire sauce and garlic powder. Top the beef roast with apple and onion. Cover slow cooker and cook on low for 5 to 6 hours or until the meat is tender. Remove the beef roast and onion. Let cool for 15 minutes before slicing. Into a medium saucepan, strain cooking liquid and discard apple. Bring cooking liquid to a boil and heat until reduced to 2 cups, about 15 minutes. In a medium bowl, combine cornstarch and cold water, mixing until smooth. Stir in browning sauce. Add cornstarch mixture to cooking liquid and bring to a boil. Cook and stir for 2 minutes or until thick. Pour mixture over roast and serve.

GLAZED APRICOT CHICKEN

2 boneless, skinless chicken
   breast halves
¼ C. apricot fruit spread
1 ½ tsp. soy sauce

1 tsp. Dijon mustard
1 tsp. honey
1 tsp. margarine, melted

Preheat broiler. On a broiler pan coated with nonstick cooking spray, place chicken breast halves. In a medium bowl, combine apricot fruit spread, soy sauce, Dijon mustard, honey and melted margarine. Brush half the apricot mixture over each chicken breast half. Place chicken 5" to 6" under broiler for 5 minutes. Turn chicken over and brush with remaining apricot mixture. Broil chicken until juices run clear.

Tantalizing Turkey Tortilla Bake

1 small onion, finely chopped
½ tsp. garlic powder
1 tsp. vegetable oil
1 lb. ground turkey
1 T. vinegar
2 tsp. chili powder
1 ½ tsp. dried oregano
½ tsp. cumin
¼ tsp. cayenne pepper

1 (15 oz.) can black beans, rinsed and drained
1 (16 oz.) jar salsa
¾ C. chicken broth
8 (8″) tortillas
½ C. shredded Monterey Jack cheese
⅓ C. sour cream

Preheat oven to 350º. In a skillet over medium heat, sauté chopped onion and garlic powder in oil until onion is tender. Add ground turkey, vinegar, chili powder, dried oregano, cumin and cayenne pepper. Cook and stir until turkey is no longer pink. Stir in black beans. Remove turkey mixture from heat. In a small bowl, combine salsa and chicken broth. In a 2½-quart greased baking dish, spread a thin layer of salsa mixture on the bottom. Cut tortillas into 1″ strips and then into thirds. Arrange half the tortilla strips over salsa mixture. Top with half the turkey mixture and half the remaining salsa mixture. Repeat layers. Sprinkle Monterey Jack cheese over top of the casserole. Cover and bake for 25 minutes until bubbly. Cut into square pieces and top each serving with sour cream.

CHEESEBURGER SOUP

1 lb. ground beef
½ C. chopped onion
3 C. water
1 (10 ¾ oz.) can Cheddar
   cheese soup, diluted

1 (10 ¾ oz.) can tomato soup
3 T. dill pickle relish
1 C. uncooked small shell pasta
Ketchup and mustard to taste

In a large saucepan over medium heat, cook ground beef and chopped onion until meat is no longer pink, drain saucepan and stir in water, Cheddar cheese soup, tomato soup and dill pickle relish. Bring to a boil. Reduce to low heat and add small shell pasta. Cook, uncovered, for 15 to 20 minutes or until pasta is tender, stirring occasionally. Using a ladle, transfer soup to serving bowls and drizzle each serving with ketchup and mustard.

FUN FAST FACTS

The ancient Egyptians thought onions kept evil spirits away. When they took an oath, they placed one hand on an onion.

SOUPER SLOPPY JOES

1 lb. ground beef
1 (10 ¾ oz.) can cream of
    mushroom soup
1 T. onion soup mix

1 C. shredded
    Cheddar cheese
8 hamburger buns, split

In a medium saucepan over medium heat, cook ground beef until no longer pink. Drain saucepan and stir in cream of mushroom soup and onion soup mix. Cook beef mixture until heated throughout. Stir in shredded Cheddar cheese until melted. Place ⅓ cup of the Sloppy Joe mix over each bun and serve.

Noodles Galore Soup

¾ lb. boneless, skinless chicken breasts, cubed
2 medium carrots, sliced
1 small onion, chopped
2 celery stalks, sliced
1 clove garlic, minced
5 C. water
¼ tsp. pepper
2 (3 oz.) pkgs. chicken-flavored Ramen noodles

In a large saucepan coated with nonstick cooking spray, sauté cubed chicken, carrots, onion, celery and garlic until chicken is no longer pink. Add water, pepper and seasoning packets from the Ramen noodles. Bring to a boil. Reduce to low heat, cover and simmer for 15 to 20 minutes or until carrots are tender. Break Ramen noodles into pieces and add to soup. Cover and cook for 3 minutes or until tender.

TOASTY APPLE AND CHEESE SANDWICHES

6 slices bread
2 T. mayonnaise
6 slices Cheddar cheese
1 medium tart apple, peeled,
   cored and cut crosswise
   into 6 rings

1 T. brown sugar
12 bacon strips, cooked
   and drained

Preheat broiler. On a baking sheet pan, place the slices of bread and toast one side under broiler for 2 minutes. Spread mayonnaise on the untoasted side of each bread slice. Top 3 slices of bread with a Cheddar cheese slice, apple ring and sprinkle with brown sugar. Cross 2 strips of bacon over each sandwich. Broil in the oven 6" from the heat for 2 to 3 minutes or until cheese melts. Place the remaining 3 slices of bread on top of each sandwich, toasted side out.

SWEET CITRUS CHICKEN SANDWICH

6 boneless, skinless chicken
  breast halves
¼ C. orange juice
¼ C. lemon juice
¼ C. honey
2 T. vegetable oil
1 T. mustard
¼ tsp. poultry seasoning

⅛-¼ tsp. cayenne pepper
6 slices Monterey Jack cheese,
  optional
6 Kaiser rolls, split
6 thin tomato slices
6 red onion slices
  Shredded lettuce

On a hard flat surface, pound chicken until uniform in thickness and set aside. In a 9 x 13″ baking dish, combine orange juice, lemon juice, honey, vegetable oil, mustard, poultry seasoning and cayenne pepper. Place chicken breasts in mixture and turn over to coat. Cover the baking dish and chill in the refrigerator for 6 to 8 hours. Drain the chicken breast and discard the marinade. Cook on the grill over medium heat, uncovered, for 10 to 12 minutes, turning occasionally. Top each chicken breast with a slice of Monterey Jack cheese and grill 2 minutes until cheese begins to melt. Serve each chicken breast on a Kaiser roll topped with tomato, onion and lettuce.

TERIYAKI TURKEY BURGER

1 egg
½ C. dry bread crumbs
3 green onions, chopped
4 T. teriyaki sauce, divided
¼ tsp. onion powder

1 lb. ground turkey
1 (8 oz.) can sliced
    pineapple, drained
4 hamburger buns

In a large bowl, combine egg, bread crumbs, chopped green onions, 3 tablespoons teriyaki sauce and onion powder. Crumble ground turkey over mixture and stir. Shape turkey mixture into four ¾″ thick patties. Preheat grill and coat grill rack with nonstick cooking spray. Over medium heat, cook turkey patties, covered, for 6 to 8 minutes on each side. Brush turkey patties with remaining 1 tablespoon teriyaki sauce during the last 5 minutes. Grill pineapple slices for 4 minutes on each side or until heated throughout. Serve turkey burgers and pineapple on buns.

CITRUS PORK ROAST

1 medium grapefruit
1 medium orange
1 medium lemon
2 T. olive oil
1 ½ tsp. crushed dried rosemary

½ tsp. salt
1 clove garlic, minced
1 (5 lb.) boneless pork loin
  roast, trimmed

Preheat oven to 325°. Cut grapefruit, orange and lemon in half. In a small bowl, squeeze fruit to remove juice, reserving the rinds. In a large resealable plastic bag, combine fruit juice mixture, olive oil, crushed rosemary, salt and minced garlic. Make shallow cuts in top of pork loin roast. Place roast in the bag, seal and turn to coat. Chill in refrigerator overnight. In a shallow baking pan, place roast and marinade. Bake, uncovered, for 1 ½ hours, basting with juices every 30 minutes. Slice fruit rinds into ¼" strips and arrange around roast. Bake 30 minutes longer or until internal temperature of roast reads 160° on a meat thermometer. Let stand for 15 minutes before slicing. Arrange pork slices on a platter and drizzle with ¼ cup of pan juices.

MY OWN MUNCHIES

Little Recipes for Little Cooks

Little Recipes for Little Cooks

Allowing children to help in the kitchen is a fun, educational experience and a great way to spend time as a family. Before creating these yummy kid-friendly recipes, make sure everyone understands these few rules to prevent accidents and illnesses from occuring.

1. Always wash hands before handling food.

2. Wash all fruits and vegetables before eating.

3. Put foods like milk, yogurt, lunch meat and eggs back in the refrigerator right away.

4. Children should never handle sharp utensils themselves. Adult supervision is a must to prevent serious injuries. If children insist on preparing snacks themselves, have fruit and vegetables precut and waiting in the refrigerator so they are ready to roll when the bug to bake arises.

5. If a recipe requires the oven or stovetop, make sure children know an adult must help with this particular step in the directions. In addition, always turn the handles of pots and pans inward while on the stovetop so children can't reach them.

CLASSIC ANTS ON A LOG

5 celery stalks　　　　　　　¼ C. raisins
½ C. peanut butter

Cut celery stalks in half. Spread each celery stalk with peanut butter. Sprinkle raisins over celery stalks and serve.

LADYBUGS

2 red apples
¼ C. raisins

1 T. peanut butter
8 thin pretzel sticks

Slice apples in half and remove the core. On a small plate, place each apple flat-side-down. Dab peanut butter on the back of each apple or "lady bug," then attach raisins onto each peanut butter dab as dots. Dab peanut butter on the front of the apple and attach raisins as eyes. Press 2 pretzel sticks into each apple to make antennae.

AWESOME OYSTERS

1 (1 oz.) pkg. ranch
   dressing mix
½ tsp. dried dillweed
¼ C. vegetable oil
¼ tsp. lemon pepper
¼ tsp. garlic powder
5 C. oyster crackers

Preheat oven to 250°. In a large bowl, combine the dressing mix, dillweed, vegetable oil, lemon pepper and garlic powder. Add oyster crackers to the mixture and toss to coat. Spread the mixture evenly on a baking sheet. Bake for 15 to 20 minutes, stirring occasionally.

Peanut Towers

2 slices white bread

2 T. butter

4 T. peanut butter

1 tsp. white sugar

1 slice whole wheat bread

Spread butter over 1 slice of white bread. Spread peanut butter on the bread over the layer of butter. Sprinkle sugar over the top of the peanut butter layer. Place a slice of wheat bread on top of the white bread and repeat the layering of butter, peanut butter and sugar. Top the wheat bread slice with a slice of white bread. Cut the layered slices into 9 pieces. Insert toothpicks into each piece and serve.

WRAP UP BANANAS

1 (6") tortilla

2 T. peanut butter

1 T. honey

1 banana, peeled

2 T. raisins

Lay tortilla flat. Spread peanut butter and honey over tortilla. Place banana in the middle and sprinkle with raisins. Wrap up and serve.

FUN FAST FACTS

There is more fiber in an orange than almost any other fruit or vegetable.

BANANA POPSICLES

4 large bananas

2 C. fruit-flavored yogurt

1 C. crushed cereal, any kind

4 Popsicle sticks

Peel and dip whole banana in the fruit-flavored yogurt. On a plate, place the crushed cereal. Roll bananas in the crushed cereal to coat. Insert a Popsicle stick into the bottom of each banana. Chill in the freezer until firm.

APPLE SMILES

1 apple

2 T. peanut butter

4 mini marshmallows

Cut the apple into 16 slices. For each "smile," spread peanut butter on one side of 2 apple slices. Place 4 mini marshmallows on one apple slice as teeth and top with the other slice.

CRISPY CHEESE BALLS

1 C. shredded
 Cheddar cheese
1 C. crushed cereal, any kind

¼ C. butter
½ C. flour

Preheat oven to 375°. In a medium bowl, mix together shredded Cheddar cheese, crushed cereal, butter and flour. Form the mixture in several little balls. On a baking sheet, evenly space the cheese balls and bake for 10 minutes.

APPLE ROLL-UPS

1 (8 oz.) tube crescent rolls
1 apple, sliced
1 tsp. cinnamon and
    sugar mixture

1 T. orange juice

Preheat oven to 375°. On a baking sheet, separate crescent rolls into triangles. Place an apple slice in the larger end of the each triangle. Sprinkle some of the cinnamon and sugar mixture over each and then roll up. Drizzle each crescent roll with orange juice. Bake for 15 to 17 minutes or according to the directions on the crescent roll package.

VEGETABLE PARFAIT

¼ C. ranch dressing

3 to 4 grape tomatoes

3 to 4 cucumber slices

¼ C. mushrooms

5 radishes

¼ C. shredded carrots

¼ C. broccoli florets

¼ C. cauliflower florets

¼ C. peas

In a parfait or tall glass, drizzle some of the ranch dressing. Lay grape tomatoes over the dressing. Drizzle more ranch dressing over the tomatoes. Then, lay cucumber slices on top and drizzle with dressing again. Repeat this layering process using mushrooms, radishes, shredded carrots, broccoli florets, cauliflower florets, peas and the remain ranch dressing.

FUN FAST FACTS

Tomatoes are high in carotenoids. Eating foods with carotenoids can lower the risk of cancer.

EASY PUDDINGSICLES

6 popsicle sticks
1 (pkg. of 6) ready to eat pudding
   or gelatin snacks

Insert one popsicle stick through the foil of each pudding or gelatin container. Chill in the freezer until pudding or gelatin is firm. Remove Puddingsicles from the freezer and run warm water over plastic to loosen the container. Peel off cover before serving.

HOMEMADE ANIMAL CRACKERS

½ C. rolled oats
¾ C. flour
¼ tsp. baking soda
¼ tsp. salt

¼ C. butter
2 tsp. honey
¼ C. buttermilk

Preheat oven to 400°. In a blender or food processor, grind oats until fine. In a medium bowl, stir together the blended oats, flour, baking soda and salt. Cut the butter in ½″ cubes and stir into the oat mixture until there are no lumps. Stir in the buttermilk and honey to form a stiff dough. On a lightly floured surface, roll the dough out to ⅛″ thickness. Cut into desired shapes with small cookie cutters. Place cookies 1″ apart onto lightly greased baking sheets. Bake for 5 to 7 minute, until edges are lightly browned. Remove from baking sheets and cool on wire racks.

SPECIAL DISHES FOR SUPER KIDS

Recipes for kids with diabetes,
dairy and nut allergies

Fast facts on kids who require special diets

Some children have special dietary needs aside from making sure they're gobbling up all the recommended food groups.

About one in every 400 to 600 children and adolescents have Type 1 diabetes. Type 1 diabetes is when the body does not produce insulin, which is needed to take sugar (glucose) from the blood to the cells. With a condition like diabetes, eating well-balanced meals helps to keep the blood glucose level as close to normal (non-diabetes level) as possible. Diabetics may need to pay extra attention to the amount of carbohydrates they eat to maintain control of their blood sugar level.

Food allergies can also make meal time a bit difficult for some families. According to the U.S. FDA, nearly six percent of children age three and under in the United States have food allergies. Two of the most common allergens are eggs and cow's milk, both of which are ingredients in many kid-friendly foods.

Special diets should always be discussed with a physician before trying anything new. With that in mind, this section of Vegetables Schmegetables is dedicated to helping families find yummy alternatives to fit their special diet needs.

TOO YUMMY TOMATO BASIL PIZZA

Great for kids with diabetes or nut allergies

½ whole wheat English muffin

2 T. no-added sodium tomato sauce

2 T. part-skim shredded mozzarella cheese

2 T. diced tomato

1 T. fresh chopped basil

Preheat broiler. Place whole wheat English muffin on a small baking sheet. Spread tomato sauce on top of muffin. Top with cheese. Sprinkle diced tomato and fresh basil over cheese. Place on baking sheet under broiler until cheese is browned. Serve immediately.

TASTY TACO POPCORN

Great for kids with diabetes or dairy allergies

7 ½ C. air-popped popcorn
Butter-flavored cooking spray
1 ½ tsp. cumin
1 ½ tsp. garlic powder

1 ½ tsp. onion powder
Cayenne pepper, optional
1 ½ tsp. Worcestershire sauce

Preheat oven to 300°. In a large bowl, lightly coat the popcorn with butter-flavored cooking spray. Toss popcorn to coat evenly. In a medium bowl, combine cumin, garlic powder, onion powder and cayenne pepper. Sprinkle spice mixture over popcorn and toss to coat evenly. Drizzle Worcestershire sauce over popcorn and toss once more. On large baking pans, spread popcorn out evenly. Bake for 10 minutes, tossing once after 5 minutes. Let popcorn cool before serving.

WRAP IT UP

Great for kids with diabetes or nut allergies

1 low-fat whole wheat tortilla
2 T. light cream cheese
1 large lettuce leaf
1 (1 oz.) lean and low-sodium
  turkey slice

1 (1 oz.) lean and low-sodium
  ham slice
1 (1 oz.) Swiss cheese slice
2 to 3 tomato slices

Place the tortilla on a flat surface. Spread light cream cheese over one side of tortilla. Place lettuce leaf, turkey slice, ham slice, Swiss cheese and tomato slices on top of the cream cheese. Roll tortilla into a cylinder. Slice the wrap in half and serve.

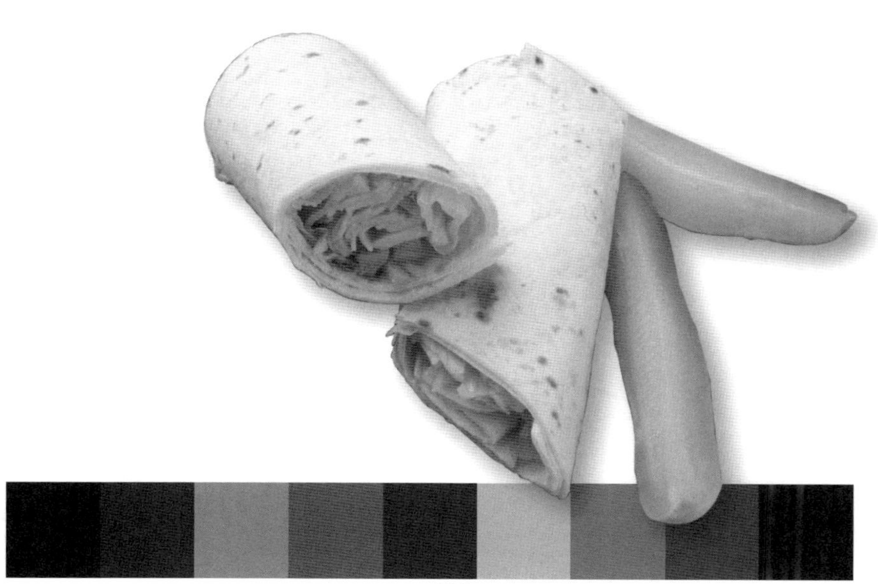

TANGY TURKEY TENDERLOIN WITH VEGGIES

Great for kids with diabetes or dairy allergies

1 ½ tsp. ground cumin

3 cloves garlic, minced

1 lb. boneless, skinless
   turkey breast tenderloin

2 T. red wine vinegar

2 tsp. sugar substitute
   with sucralose

2 tsp. cornstarch

1 C. chopped tomatoes

½ C. chopped zucchini

½ C. chopped yellow squash

½ C. chopped onion

2 T. chopped cilantro

1 T. chopped jalapeno pepper

Preheat broiler. In a small bowl, combine ground cumin and minced garlic. Rub the mixture on both sides of turkey breast tenderloin. Broil the turkey breast tenderloin for 5 minutes on both sides until juices run clear. In a medium saucepan, combine red wine vinegar, sugar substitute and cornstarch. Mix until smooth. Stir in chopped tomatoes, zucchini, yellow squash, onion, cilantro and jalapeno pepper. Place saucepan over medium heat and cook, stirring often, until mixture boils and thickens. Continue to cook and stir for 2 minutes after mixture thickens. Remove the turkey from the oven and place on a plate. Spoon vegetable mixture over turkey and serve.

YOGURT DELIGHT TO GO

Great for kids with diabetes or nut allergies

⅓ C. sliced peaches, canned in light syrup

¾ C. fat-free yogurt, any fruit flavor

1 T. dried cranberries

⅓ C. oat bran

In a 16-ounce plastic cup, place peach slices. Pour yogurt over peaches. Sprinkle dried cranberries over yogurt and top with oat bran. Serve immediately or cover and refrigerate until ready to serve.

FUN FAST FACTS

There are more than 100 different cranberry varieties, many of which were named after the families that first planted them.

WHOLE WHEAT DAIRY-FREE PANCAKES

Great for kids with diabetes or dairy allergies

2 C. whole wheat pastry flour
¼ C. wheat germ
3 T. soy flour
2 T. sugar
4 tsp. baking powder

½ tsp. salt
3 eggs
¼ C. vegetable oil
¼ tsp. almond extract
2 C. soy milk

Preheat griddle to 350°. In a large mixing bowl, combine whole wheat pastry flour, wheat germ, soy flour, sugar, baking powder and salt. In another large mixing bowl, whisk together eggs, vegetable oil and almond extract. Stir in soy milk. Combine the two mixtures. Batter should be slightly thick. For each pancake, pour ¼ cup batter onto the griddle. Cook pancakes until edges look dry and bubbles burst. Flip and cook 1 minute until golden brown.

STRAWBERRY SPINACH SALAD

Great for kids with diabetes

3 T. red wine vinegar

3 T. orange juice

1 ½ T. vegetable oil

¼ tsp. dry mustard

⅓ tsp. poppy seeds

6 C. fresh torn spinach pieces

½ C. mandarin oranges

1 C. sliced strawberries

¼ C. cashews

½ C. soy blue cheese crumbles

In a medium bowl, mix together red wine vinegar, orange juice, vegetable oil, dry mustard and poppy seeds. In a large bowl, toss together spinach, mandarin oranges and sliced strawberries. Pour the dressing mixture over salad and toss to coat evenly. Sprinkle cashews and soy blue cheese over each serving.

MAC MINUS CHEESE

Great for kids with diabetes or dairy allergies

1 (8 oz.) pkg. uncooked
  elbow macaroni
1 T. vegetable oil
1 medium onion, chopped
1 C. cashews
⅓ C. lemon juice
1 ⅓ C. water

Salt to taste
⅓ C. vegetable oil
1 (4 oz.) can roasted
  red peppers, drained
3 T. nutritional yeast
1 tsp. garlic powder
1 tsp. onion powder

Preheat oven to 350°. In a large pot over medium heat, bring lightly salted water to a boil. Add macaroni and cook for 8 to 10 minutes or until al dente and drain. Transfer cooked macaroni to a medium baking dish. In a medium saucepan over medium heat, place vegetable oil. Stir in chopped onion. Cook until tender and lightly browned. Mix the onion gently with the macaroni. In a blender or food processor, blend cashews, lemon juice, water and salt. Add vegetable oil, roasted red peppers, nutritional yeast, garlic powder and onion powder. Blend until smooth. Add blended mixture to macaroni and onions and mix thoroughly. Bake for 45 minutes or until lightly browned. Cool for 10 to 15 minutes before serving.

SWEET AND SOUR COOL SLAW

Great for kids with dairy allergies

½ C. sugar
½ C. cider vinegar
¼ C. cold water
1 tsp. salt
½ tsp. mustard seed

½ tsp. celery seed
8 C. shredded cabbage
½ C. chopped celery
½ C. chopped green pepper
1 T. chopped pimento pepper

In a jar with a tight-fitting lid, combine sugar, cider vinegar, cold water, salt, mustard seed and celery seed. Cover jar tightly and shake vigorously until sugar is dissolved. Chill dressing in the refrigerator for several hours or overnight. In a large bowl, toss together shredded cabbage, chopped celery, chopped green pepper, chopped pimento and dressing mixture until evenly coated. Cover and chill in the refrigerator until ready to serve.

CRANBERRY BUBBLY

Great for kids with diabetes, nut or dairy allergies

½ C. ice cubes

7 oz. diet lemon-lime soda

3 oz. cranberry juice cocktail

Fill a tall glass with ice cubes. Pour in cranberry juice cocktail and diet lemon lime soda. Stir with a long spoon and serve.

FUN FAST FACTS

In the U.S., cranberries are consumed the most during Thanksgiving and Christmas.

Tooty Fruity Recipes

Veggies Schmeggies

Snappy Snacks

Brainy Breakfast

Sandwich Standouts and Marvelous Main Dishes

My Own Munchies

Special Dishes for Super Kids